# First World War
## and Army of Occupation
# War Diary
## France, Belgium and Germany

35 DIVISION
106 Infantry Brigade,
Brigade Trench Mortar Battery
1 July 1916 - 31 July 1916

WO95/2490/7

The Naval & Military Press Ltd
www.nmarchive.com
Published in association with The National Archives

Published by

## The Naval & Military Press Ltd

Unit 10 Ridgewood Industrial Park,

Uckfield, East Sussex,

TN22 5QE England

Tel: +44 (0) 1825 749494

www.naval-military-press.com

www.nmarchive.com

*This diary has been reprinted in facsimile from the original. Any imperfections are inevitably reproduced and the quality may fall short of modern type and cartographic standards.*

© **Crown Copyright**
**Images reproduced by permission of The National Archives, London, England, 2015.**

# Contents

| Document type | Place/Title | Date From | Date To |
|---|---|---|---|
| Heading | WO95/2490/7 | | |
| Heading | 35th Division 106th Infy Bde 106th Trench Mortar Bty Jly 1916 | | |
| War Diary | | 01/07/1916 | 31/07/1916 |

Noas/2490/7

35TH DIVISION
106TH INFY BDE

106TH TRENCH MORTAR BTY

JLY 1916

35 July
Army Form C. 2118
Vol 1

# WAR DIARY
## of 106th T.M. Battery
## INTELLIGENCE SUMMARY

(Erase heading not required.)

| Place | Date | Hour | Summary of Events and Information | Remarks and references to Appendices |
|---|---|---|---|---|
| | July 1st | | On route from LAVENTIE to the South. | |
| | 3rd | 3·0 a.m. | Marched from BAIELLEU AUX CORNAILLES to IVERGNY. Had a Motor Lorry to move our guns. | |
| | 5th | 7·0 p.m. | Marched from IVERGNY to AUTHIE. From this date onwards could not procure a Motor Lorry. | |
| | 10th | 2·15 p.m. | Marched from AUTHIE to VARENNES. | |
| | 12th | 9·0 p.m. | Marched from VARENNES to BRESLE. | |
| | 13th | 10·0 a.m. | Marched from BRESLE to BOIS LES CELESTINS | |
| | 13th | 6 p.m. | " " BOIS LES CELESTINS to BILLON COPSE | |
| | 14th | 11·45 a.m. | " " BILLON COPSE to TALUS BOISÉ | |
| | 15th | 1·0 p.m. | Moved up to MONTAUBAN in support to 3rd Division. | |
| | 19th | 10·0 p.m. | Moved from TALUS BOISÉ to CAFTET WOOD | |
| | 24th | 1·30 a.m. | Moved up CAFTET WOOD to Valley between MONTAUBAN and LONGUEVAL. in support to 30th Division. | |
| | 25th | 6·30 p.m. | Left MONTAUBAN for CAFTET WOOD | |
| | 29th | 8·30 p.m. | Left CAFTET WOOD for Trenches near GERMANS WOOD in support to the 89th Bde. for the attack on GUILLEMONT. | |
| | 30th | 4·0 a.m. | Moved further forward to DUBLIN TRENCH. | |
| | 31st | 11·15 p.m. | Moved back from DUBLIN TRENCH to CAFTET WOOD. | |

Rad Radwick Capt.
O.C. 106 T.M.B.

www.ingramcontent.com/pod-product-compliance
Lightning Source LLC
Chambersburg PA
CBHW081254170426
43191CB00037B/2154